AN IDEAS INTO ACTION GUIDEBOOK

Influence

Gaining Commitment, Getting Results

IDEAS INTO ACTION GUIDEBOOKS

Aimed at managers and executives who are concerned with their own and others' development, each guidebook in this series gives specific advice on how to complete a developmental task or solve a leadership problem.

LEAD CONTRIBUTORS	David Baldwin
	Curt Grayson
CONTRIBUTORS	Kate Beatty
	Rich Hughes
	Gene Klann
GUIDEBOOK ADVISORY GROUP	Victoria A. Guthrie
	Cynthia D. McCauley
	Ellen Van Velsor
DIRECTOR OF PUBLICATIONS	Martin Wilcox
EDITOR	Peter Scisco
ASSOCIATE EDITOR	Karen Mayworth
DESIGN AND LAYOUT	Joanne Ferguson
CONTRIBUTING ARTISTS	Laura J. Gibson
	Chris Wilson, 29 & Company

CCL No. 424
ISBN-10: 1-882197-82-8
ISBN-13: 978-1-882197-82-8

CENTER FOR CREATIVE LEADERSHIP
POST OFFICE BOX 26300
GREENSBORO, NORTH CAROLINA 27438-6300
336-288-7210
WWW.CCL.ORG / PUBLICATIONS

AN IDEAS INTO ACTION GUIDEBOOK

Influence
Gaining Commitment, Getting Results

David Baldwin and Curt Grayson

Center for
Creative
Leadership

NORTH AMERICA EUROPE ASIA

www.ccl.org

This series of guidebooks draws on the practical knowledge that the Center for Creative Leadership (CCL®) has generated in the course of more than thirty years of research and educational activity conducted in partnership with hundreds of thousands of managers and executives. Much of this knowledge is shared—in a way that is distinct from the typical university department, professional association, or consultancy. CCL is not simply a collection of individual experts, although the individual credentials of its staff are impressive; rather it is a community, with its members holding certain principles in common and working together to understand and generate practical responses to today's leadership and organizational challenges.

The purpose of the series is to provide managers with specific advice on how to complete a developmental task or solve a leadership challenge. In doing that, the series carries out CCL's mission to advance the understanding, practice, and development of leadership for the benefit of society worldwide. We think you will find the Ideas Into Action Guidebooks an important addition to your leadership toolkit.

Table of Contents

EXECUTIVE BRIEF

Influence is an essential component of leadership. Your position in an organization and the power it gives you aren't always enough to motivate people to do what you ask. Developing your influence skills can help you gain commitment from people at all levels: direct reports, peers, and bosses.

This book includes an assessment tool to help you determine the influence tactics you currently use. Some tactics depend on logic, others appeal to emotions, and others are cooperative appeals. You may discover tactics you rarely use, and you can develop those tactics to become more effective.

You will learn what to do before, during, and after an influence session. Every influence attempt can become a learning experience, and you can continue to enhance this crucial leadership capability.

What Is Influence?

Influence is an essential component of leadership. You need it to sell ideas and to motivate people to support and implement decisions—sometimes your own ideas and decisions, and sometimes those of others that you represent. Your position in an organization and the power it gives you may not be enough to influence people and motivate them to complete a task. Contemporary organizations have adopted flexible and interactive structures that rely less on hierarchy and more on a leader's ability to influence and win commitment. Influence is important because it achieves desirable outcomes. Leaders can strategically use their influence skills to communicate their vision, to align the efforts of others in the organization, and to build commitment to the work.

Leaders who are able to effectively utilize their influence skills can achieve their goals and objectives more successfully. But what does it mean to effectively use your influence skills? To understand the answer to that question, you need to know that the use of influence tactics can produce three distinctly different outcomes: resistance, compliance, and commitment.

The least desirable outcome of your trying to influence others is resistance to the request you are making. People may directly oppose what you're asking for or use a stealthy resistance, perhaps sabotaging your efforts to influence in subtle ways. For example, they may initially agree with your request, but then put roadblocks in the way of its completion or make excuses about why it cannot be accomplished.

Compliance is better than resistance, but it's far from an ideal response. The person you're trying to influence will carry out your request, but with minimal effort and little if any acceptance of the reasons you have given to gain support. Compliance may be

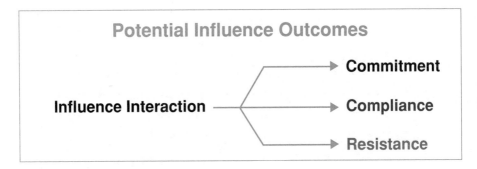

sufficient if the request is simple and routine and doesn't require the other person to exert much additional energy or effort to accomplish it. But it's important to remember that although you can get people to act in productive ways by getting their compliance, you don't change their attitude toward the work itself.

When your influence efforts result in commitment, you have succeeded in presenting sufficient reasons to secure voluntary endorsement and support for carrying out a task. This is an important distinction, and it's vital if what you are asking requires other people to take on jobs that may not be simple, quick, or without cost to their personal time or work schedules. When you are able to influence someone to the level of commitment, you receive several advantages:

- There's less need to monitor progress toward your goals or fight resistance to them.
- There is greater sustained effort, which is particularly important when the tasks involved are complex or difficult and require a concentrated effort over a long period of time.
- Committed people endorse your objectives, and so tend to be more efficient, creative, resilient, and focused toward your shared goal.
- Working relationships improve.

Developing influence skills can help you achieve commitment from your peers, your direct reports, and your bosses. These groups often require different approaches for influence tactics to be successful. Whether you attempt to influence a key individual, a specific group, or whole departments, you should consider individual personalities, goals and objectives, and organizational roles and responsibilities as the first step toward getting commitment.

Whom Do You Influence?

Organizational leaders, professional managers, and different work units often describe various stakeholder groups as critical to their success in putting influence to work on and off the job. Each of these groups has special concerns and issues. They often have their own agendas and their own perspectives and priorities.

It's not unusual for managers to find themselves in an ongoing struggle to learn how to influence different stakeholders. Sometimes they have to "influence up" in presenting ideas to their bosses or other superiors. Sometimes they have to build partnerships with peers across organizational boundaries. And there is always the challenge of motivating direct reports. Providing specific rules for how to influence each of these groups is nearly impossible, because each manager's situation is different. Some organizations create a collegial atmosphere with open communication and broad collaboration, while other organizations are more politically driven and focused on individual star performers.

One boss might give a manager an enormous amount of freedom to design and control a team's work and schedule, while another boss in a different organization exerts more direct control. Peer relationships also span a wide range. Some peers work together on projects and have overlapping responsibilities, while others have more indirect relationships and little interaction. Managers are also likely to find wide differences in how direct reports

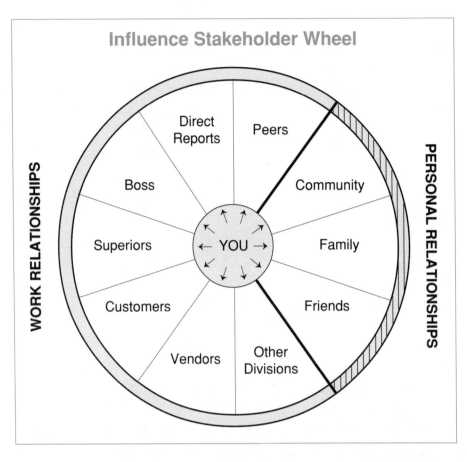

Influence Stakeholder Wheel

WORK RELATIONSHIPS

PERSONAL RELATIONSHIPS

Direct Reports

Peers

Boss

Community

Superiors

← YOU →

Family

Customers

Friends

Vendors

Other Divisions

can be successfully influenced. Some direct reports need guidance and hands-on direction, while others are capable of working more independently or collaboratively and prefer to do so.

As you consider your own situation and the cases in which you will need to draw upon your influence skills, also consider how much interpersonal power you have with those you are attempting to influence. Two types of interpersonal power are personal power and positional power. *Personal power* refers to the level of trust, respect, and relational commitment you have with another person. *Positional power* refers to the organizational power given through title or specific responsibility.

How Do You Influence?

Understanding your own influencing style is critical to your success. The first step in that understanding is an assessment of the influence tactics you currently use. You can make that assessment by using the worksheet on pages 12–14 and then round out your self-assessment by asking others for feedback.

There are three parts to the worksheet. Part 1 helps you identify and measure the most common ways you influence others. In Part 2 you will score your responses. In Part 3 you will plot your responses on a graph to show which influence tactics you can develop to be more effective.

Influence Tactics

Your measurement of the influence tactics you use most often is a reflection of your strengths and weaknesses in this area. It's important to note that most of the time when you make a simple request, people are likely to carry it out provided that it doesn't negatively affect them. If your request is clearly legitimate, relevant to their work, and something they know how to do, resistance will probably be minimal. Selecting and developing sophisticated influence tactics becomes more important when your request is perceived as unpleasant, inconvenient, and not without some sacrifice. If it's not immediately obvious to other people that complying with your request is necessary, it can be particularly difficult to influence their actions toward that end.

As you review the graph from the worksheet on pages 12–14, keep in mind that you can choose tactics that depend on logic, that appeal to emotions, or that support a cooperative effort. As a

Your Strength of Influence: A Self-Guided Worksheet

Part 1

Respond to the statements below, which describe typical actions taken to influence another person to take an action or perform a task. As you respond to the statements, don't be too concerned at this point about whether the person is a direct report, peer, boss, or other key stakeholder.

Using the scale below, please rate each statement by darkening the appropriate number.

> 1 = Almost never
> 2 = Seldom
> 3 = Sometimes
> 4 = Often
> 5 = Almost always

Q1 I objectively and logically explain to the person ① ② ③ ④ ⑤
the reason for the requested action.

Q2 I explain how a requested action, which may ① ② ③ ④ ⑤
require additional work in the person's schedule, is likely to have long-term benefits to the
person's career.

Q3 I show the person how the requested action ① ② ③ ④ ⑤
meets his or her individual goals and values.

Q4 I provide the necessary resources (time, staff, ① ② ③ ④ ⑤
materials, and technical support, for example)
the person needs to accomplish the task.

Q5 I ask for suggestions on how to improve a ① ② ③ ④ ⑤
tentative proposal in order to create a win-
win outcome for all parties involved.

Q6 I create coalitions with people who are in ① ② ③ ④ ⑤
support of the requested action.

Q7   I offer factual and detailed evidence that the proposal is feasible.   ① ② ③ ④ ⑤

Q8   I assist the person in gaining more visibility and a better reputation in the organization.   ① ② ③ ④ ⑤

Q9   I describe the task with enthusiasm and express confidence in the person's ability to accomplish it.   ① ② ③ ④ ⑤

Q10   I reduce the difficulty of carrying out the request by removing barriers to success.   ① ② ③ ④ ⑤

Q11   I ask the person for ideas about how to carry out the requested action, and I incorporate those ideas into the process.   ① ② ③ ④ ⑤

Q12   I tell the person about credible people who are in support of the requested action.   ① ② ③ ④ ⑤

Q13   I explain clearly and logically why the proposal is the best possible choice of all competing choices.   ① ② ③ ④ ⑤

Q14   I provide opportunities for the person to learn new skills that will be beneficial.   ① ② ③ ④ ⑤

Q15   I link my request to a clear and appealing vision the person can fully support.   ① ② ③ ④ ⑤

Q16   I volunteer to help the person accomplish the task.   ① ② ③ ④ ⑤

Q17   I thoughtfully respond to the person's concerns and suggestions.   ① ② ③ ④ ⑤

Q18   I involve credible people to help me influence the person.   ① ② ③ ④ ⑤

Q19   I explain the logical process for how potential organizational problems or concerns will be handled.   ① ② ③ ④ ⑤

Q20 I make the person's job easier or more interesting. ① ② ③ ④ ⑤

Q21 I appeal to the person's self-image. ① ② ③ ④ ⑤

Q22 I offer to help the person with his or her regular work. ① ② ③ ④ ⑤

Q23 I involve the person in the larger process of deciding how to carry out my goals. ① ② ③ ④ ⑤

Q24 I develop strategic alliances by networking with key stakeholders who will help me in developing my influence strategy. ① ② ③ ④ ⑤

Part 2

Add up the points for all your responses using the formulas below. The score for each scale will be from 4 to 20 points.

Scale 1: Q1 + Q7 + Q13 + Q19 = _____ This is your *organizational benefits* score.

Scale 2: Q2 + Q8 + Q14 + Q20 = _____ This is your *personal benefits* score.

Scale 3: Q3 + Q9 + Q15 + Q21 = _____ This is your *emotional appeals* score.

Scale 4: Q4 + Q10 + Q16 + Q22 = _____ This is your *collaboration* score.

Scale 5: Q5 + Q11 + Q17 + Q23 = _____ This is your *consultation* score.

Scale 6: Q6 + Q12 + Q18 + Q24 = _____ This is your *coalitions* score.

Part 3

Plot each of your scores on a graph and then connect the dots. You can use the graph on page 32 or download a copy at www.ccl.org/influence.

shortcut, think of these three broad groups as Head, Heart, and Hands. If you see areas in which your influence skills are under-developed, consult the descriptions below to understand what's required to make the best use of those tactics in your own situation.

Logical Appeals (Head)

These tactics appeal to other people's rational and intellectual positions. With this approach, you present an argument for the best choice of action based on two different but important types of benefits—organizational and personal—that other people gain if they agree to your proposal.

Objectively and logically explain to the person the reason for the requested action. One of the most powerful and persuasive incentives for someone to agree to your request is simply that it makes sense. This tactic relies on two critical components to minimize resistance: one, that you have done the research and the thinking prior to your attempt at influencing the person; and two, that you are able to explain your request in such a way that it comes across as a clear and compelling argument.

Offer factual and detailed evidence that the proposal is feasible. In your zeal to convince another person of your position, avoid the common tendency to overstate the benefits. Don't focus on what's possible under ideal conditions but explain benefits as they exist under real conditions.

Explain clearly and logically why the proposal is the best possible choice of all competing choices. Another compelling and influential argument is that you have thought about several different options in addition to your own. Explain that you have thoughtfully considered the advantages and disadvantages of other approaches but your plan most completely meets the objective.

Explain the logical process for how potential organizational problems or concerns will be handled. Allow people you're trying

> When Hewlett-Packard (HP) and Compaq Computer announced their planned merger in 2001, it wasn't clear to shareholders or employees what all of the benefits might be. But HP CEO Carly Fiorina was looking past the benefits to the core of the issue—survival in a high-tech world where the megaprofits of the 1990s would be replaced by slower growth. To sustain the company, she made a logical argument to employees and shareholders that huge cost savings would result from purchasing Compaq and creating a new mix of products and services from the two firms' complementary offerings. That argument contributed to a narrow win in a shareholder vote, and it proved out when HP reported more than $2.5 billion in cost savings by the end of 2003.

to influence to ask questions, indicate problems, and voice concerns they have with your proposal or idea. Listen calmly and carefully, and avoid getting defensive or interpreting their concerns or questions as resistance. Remain flexible—these might be problems or concerns you had not considered. Their concerns may be an expression of their natural anxiety in the face of the changes your proposal might bring. You will need to address that anxiety to move your ideas forward.

Explain how a requested action, which may require additional work in the person's schedule, is likely to have long-term benefits to the person's career. These days, employees place a lot of emphasis on managing their own careers. When you ask people to support your idea (an action that may require additional effort on their part), build a case for how their support may help develop their own careers.

Assist the person in gaining more visibility and a better reputation in the organization. Many people seek out high-profile projects that give them exposure to senior decision makers and create for them a better reputation in the organization. Explain that the opportunity inherent in your proposal provides a challenge that can help someone move to the next level of his or her career, but that it carries the risk of failure. Offer to provide whatever support you can so that the person will feel confident in supporting your idea and moving into a more visible position.

Provide opportunities for the person to learn new skills that will be beneficial. A motivator for some people may be to expand or learn new skills. If your proposal helps them to develop, they will be more motivated to agree with you. Support is important to successfully learning new skills, so be ready to provide it.

Make the person's job easier or more interesting. If your request can reduce the amount of stress people work under or in some other way lighten their loads, they are more likely to support it. Some people are less concerned with their workloads than with how interesting and challenging their jobs are. If you can realistically assess that a person's motivation is linked to challenging assignments and your proposal offers such challenges, you can use that information to secure his or her commitment.

Emotional Appeals (Heart)

A second major category of influence tactics includes ideas that carry your message by relating it to an important emotional motivator. An idea that promotes a person's feelings of well-being, service, or sense of belonging has a good chance of gaining support.

Show the person how the requested action meets his or her individual goals and values. Employees come into organizations with individual goals and values that guide their lives. They are looking for alignment between the goals and values those organizations claim and their own. Present your proposal in such a way that they can see that their support helps them meet their own goals and those of the organization.

The year is 1962, and the Cold War is at its peak. Five years before, the Soviet Union had successfully launched Sputnik I, a 184-pound aluminum ball that emitted radio beeps as it orbited Earth. Those little beeps were the clarion call to action, and President John F. Kennedy urged America to pick up the technological gauntlet by appealing to the best side of its nature. During a speech at Rice University in Houston, Texas, Kennedy exhorted America to land a manned spacecraft on the moon and bring it safely back to Earth before the decade was out—not because it was easy, but because it was hard. He appealed to the nation's sense of historic challenges and global responsibilities. Seven years later, the goal was met.

Describe the task with enthusiasm and express confidence in the person's ability to accomplish it. It's rare to find someone who would not want to be thought of as capable and skilled. Even so, different people prefer to receive encouragement in different ways. If you can deliver your support at the right level, it will make it easier for people to support your request—either because your support gives them the confidence they need to carry it out or because they feel empowered by your giving them an assignment they must complete themselves.

Link your request to a clear and appealing vision the person can fully support. Aligning the desired action with a previously established vision can provide the motivation the person needs to carry out your request.

Appeal to the person's self-image. Self-image is a powerful force. If your request puts a person in a position that doesn't fit his or her self-image, you will encounter resistance. It's important to understand the impact (positive or negative) of your request on the person's self-image. If the impact is positive, show the person that carrying out the activity is in line with that self-image. If the impact is negative, people may still be willing to follow through with your request if they see it as a temporary setback to their self-image and believe that the end result is better for them in the long run.

Cooperative Appeals (Hands)

To influence successfully, you need to do more than appeal to a person's head and heart. The power of cooperative appeals is that they build a connection between you, the person you are trying to influence, and others to get support for your proposal. Working together to accomplish a mutually important goal extends a hand to others in the organization and is an extremely effective way of influencing. Further, it illustrates the fact that influence is not always a linear process, flowing from one person to another. Instead, it is often reciprocal—flowing back and forth and yielding ideas, plans, and decisions that are better than either person's original ones.

Provide the necessary resources (time, staff, materials, and technical support, for example) the person needs to accomplish the task. An important factor in whether someone will carry out your proposal is whether you are willing and able to provide the help needed to accomplish the task. Often what you have to offer depends on your position and access, but the more you can offer, the more likely the person is to follow through with your request.

Reduce the difficulty of carrying out the request by removing barriers to success. Part of supporting a person who has agreed to take on a task is removing barriers to success or reducing the difficulty of carrying out your request. It's important for people you're trying to influence to see that you're working on their behalf.

Volunteer to help the person accomplish the task. By doing so, you model your motivation and genuine interest in the success of the project, and the person will be more likely to support you.

A sergeant supervised a team of four people. One weekend he came into the office and moved everyone's desk into a format that he thought would be more efficient. When his team came to work Monday morning, all four were really upset—so upset that he allowed them to move everything back to where it had been. Then he had them get together and give him a recommendation on how the office could be redone to make it more efficient. Interestingly enough, they came up with the same plan! So they moved the furniture back to where their supervisor had placed it. This time they were all okay with it since it had been "their idea" and not a prescription from the boss.

Offer to help the person with his or her regular work. Pay attention to where the person might be experiencing some stress in his or her current work situation, and offer to provide support. Avoid overcommitting or trying to help in an area that is not in your sphere of expertise.

Ask for suggestions on how to improve a tentative proposal in order to create a win-win outcome for all parties involved. You may need to be flexible regarding the final outcome, but this isn't always possible. The organization may hold you responsible for a task that, when completed, impacts other people. But those people may not have been consulted as to whether the right decision was made. In these situations, it's important for you to provide whatever support you can so that you can help people align with the organization's direction.

Ask the person for ideas about how to carry out the requested action, and incorporate those ideas into the process. People are more likely to commit to an idea if they have been involved in choosing how it might be accomplished. If you do ask for input, follow through and make adjustments to your proposal to accommodate their ideas. To do this, you'll have to work closely with them to decide whether what they suggest is practical and feasible. This technique lets you guide their expectations in an open way so that the final plan is more likely to meet everyone's needs.

Thoughtfully respond to the person's concerns and suggestions. Listen. Listen. Listen. Take time to reflect on the person's concerns and suggestions. You are gathering additional data that if not attended to can possibly show up with more stakeholders down the road. Thank the person for the input.

Involve the person in the larger process of deciding how to carry out your goals. Influencing takes time. Influencing is about planting seeds and growing them. Before making a specific request, ask the person his or her opinion on the general topic. Look for situations in which you can bring up your ideas for further examination and buy-in. When you feel that the time is ripe and you have established enough buy-in by incorporating the person's feedback, share your specific request.

Create coalitions with people who are in support of the requested action. Contemporary organizations have adopted a more horizontal structure, which means that very few decisions are made without involving multiple stakeholders. As a result, building coalitions of support has become critical to success. An effective tactic is to locate and involve strategic stakeholders who are aligned with your proposal and so provide a broad base of support.

Tell the person about credible people who are in support of the requested action. Be careful about name-dropping, but when given permission, use the names of people that the person will recognize and respect, and explain why those people support your idea.

Involve credible people to help you influence the person. Which leaders in your organization do people stop and listen to? Ask those leaders to promote your ideas with public endorsements.

Develop strategic alliances by networking with key stake-holders who will help you in developing your influence strategy. Building a well-established network takes time and continual maintenance. Look at every interaction, e-mail, and public discussion as a means to that end.

Putting Influence to Work

To maximize your personal influence, you need to explore which tactics reap the most support for a specific task. At the same time, you need to tailor your influence strategy for the particular person from whom you seek that support. As you gain experience using different influence tactics, you will gain more confidence in your influencing skills.

You can build that confidence and shore up any weaknesses in your personal influence repertoire one step at a time by carefully planning each situation in which you plan to solicit the support of others. That plan can take the form of a script, through which you set out an assessment of the situation (what are you trying to accomplish?) and an assessment of stakeholders from whom you seek endorsement and support. You can also review your strengths and weaknesses for different influence tactics and anticipate what kind of reaction you are likely to get for your effort. After setting out such a plan, you can map the details of a meeting between you and the person you need to influence.

Using the information in this section, think through the actions you will take before and during an influence session. After the session, review your actions and the responses of the person you are trying to influence. Reflect on your efforts so that you can learn from your experience and use what you learn to shape future encounters.

Setting Your Goals

You are more likely to have success influencing other individuals if you establish clear goals, assess your audience, identify appropriate influence tactics, and practice them. Use the following questions to work out your thoughts on whom you need to influence and what you want to accomplish.

- Who is the person you are attempting to influence, and what position does that person occupy relative to yours (boss, peer, direct report, customer, vendor, etc.)?
- What is the situation? Why has the organization assigned this task to you? Why do you need this person's support for your idea?
- What do you want the outcome of your influence session to be?
- What benefits do you and the person you want to influence receive if you handle the situation well? What will it cost you and the person you want to influence to deal effectively with the situation?
- Assess the differences and similarities of personal and/or positional power between you and the person you want to influence. How can you leverage this power to increase your influence?

Identifying Benefits and Challenges

Each influence effort you make has benefits and challenges associated with it—in other words, things that make it easier and things that make it more difficult. For example, you may have had a negative confrontation in the past with the person you are now hoping to influence. How will you deal with the residual effect of that confrontation? On the positive side, perhaps you have some expertise in a particular area that the organization has recognized and the person you want to influence wants to gain some expertise in that area as well. By identifying existing benefits and challenges, you will be better prepared to capitalize on the benefits and address the challenges. You also increase your chances of successfully influencing the person. The worksheet on page 25 will help you determine the obstacles or challenges that exist in influencing the person. Use it also to highlight benefits you can use to increase your chances of success. Three broad areas of discussion are labeled, and you may think of other areas in which benefits and challenges exist.

Developing Your Influence Session Script

Given what you know about the person you want to influence and the situation within which you'll be trying to influence that person, you can now lay out the details of how a conversation with that person might go. Successfully influencing another person involves more than just making a request. To gain the person's commitment, you will want to engage in a dialogue—communicating your goal, explaining the benefits of joining your effort, and securing the person's endorsement.

One place to start when planning a dialogue is to identify the influence tactics that are likely to work best given what you know. Review the descriptions on pages 15–22 to choose tactics you think would be the most effective. Then turn to your assessment of your influence tactics skills. Review how you scored yourself in the worksheet on pages 12–14. Pay particular attention to the tactics that you reported using less frequently, and think about how you can develop them before your influence dialogue to increase your chance of success.

It doesn't necessarily take a lot of work to develop some of these rarely used tactics; sometimes all it takes is becoming aware of the gaps in your influence tactics toolkit and then building some of those tactics into your message. Another developmental strategy

Analyzing Benefits and Challenges Worksheet

	Benefits (positive factors)	Challenges (negative factors)
Relationship What kind of working relationship do you have with the person you want to influence? What level of trust and respect exists between the two of you? Have you worked cooperatively in the past? Was that work successful? What made it successful? Have you had or do you have a conflict with this person? What situation led to the conflict? Was it resolved? Are there lingering repercussions?		
Politics and Power Does the person you want to influence occupy a higher or lower position than you in the organization? How might that difference affect your influence strategy? Does this person have an informal kind of power in the organization based on interpersonal skills, for example, or a network of peers? How can you use those skills or that network to influence the person? What challenges do they pose for you as you attempt to influence?		
Skills and Knowledge Does the person you want to influence possess necessary technical skills and knowledge that would help accomplish your task or contribute to your proposal? Would your project gain the person recognition for the skills or knowledge? Does your project encroach on a technical area that the person regards as his or her domain?		

Based on your analysis, is your attempt to influence this person in this situation likely to result in a positive outcome?

is to evaluate the benefits you have identified and think about how you can use them to shore up the tactics you don't usually use. For example, if you are skilled at collaborating but find creating a logical rationale a challenge, perhaps you can bring others into the picture to help you develop a logical argument. You may need more practice, coaching, or research to get other tactics to the skill level you need to be an effective influencer. Your goal before starting an influence dialogue is to feel some level of confidence and comfort with the tactics you have chosen to use. The worksheet on page 27 will help you work through your plan.

Conducting Your Dialogue

Now that you have assessed your skills, described your goals, described the person you are trying to influence, and sketched the groundwork for your influencing session, you are ready to have your dialogue. Use the ideas you developed with the worksheet on page 27 to help you focus during the conversation. Effective interpersonal and communication skills are critical at this stage, and you can make good use of those skills by setting the stage for your request and by establishing a rapport with the other person.

Set the stage. Pick the right time and place for your influence dialogue. Find a setting where there will be minimal distractions. Pick a neutral site to minimize personal and positional power differences. Create an atmosphere that encourages openness, optimism, and connection with the person you are attempting to influence.

Establish rapport. Describe the situation. Check to see that the person understands what you are saying. Be mindful of the powerful impact of nonverbal communication such as body language and tone of voice. Make sure to establish eye contact, smile, and let the person know that you are listening to what he or she has to say. Watch the person's reactions as you're speaking, and capitalize on

Influence Dialogue Worksheet

Which logical appeals will be most effective?	What specifically will you say and do to use these tactics?
Which emotional appeals will be most effective?	What specifically will you say and do to use these tactics?
Which cooperative appeals will be most effective?	What specifically will you say and do to use these tactics?

Anticipate possible responses. What might the person feel or think after your attempt to influence? What might the person say?

Create your counterargument. Plan how you are going to use additional influence tactics to reply, if necessary, to the person's response.

Identify potential points of mutual agreement and use them to move toward your desired outcome. Secure agreement on your desired outcome. Establish clear steps that both of you will take to accomplish your agreed-upon goals.

End on a positive note. Express your appreciation and communicate your willingness to meet again to check on the progress being made toward the goal.

points of agreement to build momentum toward your desired outcome.

Recording and Reflecting

To increase your influence skills, it's important to learn from your experience. Each time you attempt to influence someone, even if it's just a small request, you have the opportunity to think back over the encounter and adjust your techniques and tactics. After your influence dialogue, record what happened and think through what you have learned. Use the following questions as a guide to focusing your lessons of experience.

- What went well? Describe the situation and the person's response.
- What did not go well? Describe the situation and the person's response.
- Did you get the outcome you wanted? Describe any compromises or modifications to your intended goal.
- What would you do differently next time?
- What steps did you and the other person agree to take next?
- What did you learn about yourself and your influence skills?
- What additional support can you find to develop your influence skills?

Influence over the Long Term

Influencing others isn't easy. It involves not only learning and practicing tactics but also assessing yourself as a messenger—your interpersonal and communication skills. Further, successfully influencing someone to endorse your agenda or commit to your desired goals may not happen immediately. Each individual you attempt to influence has to carefully consider the costs and benefits involved with agreeing to your position. That means that your flexibility and adaptability as a leader will be tested.

You can get better at influencing by using a mentor, colleague, or coach to help develop your skills. Look for influential people in your organization. Watch what they do and say and how they handle their opportunities to influence. Talk to them about their influence tactics and how they developed them. If you stay in touch with your own strengths and weaknesses, work to develop rarely used skills, and make every influence experience a learning opportunity, you will greatly enhance this crucial leadership capability.

Suggested Readings

Bragg, M. (1996). *Reinventing influence: How to get things done in a world without authority.* London: Financial Times-Prentice Hall.

Carnegie, D. (1982). *How to win friends and influence people* (Rev. ed.). New York: Pocket Books.

Cohen, A., & Bradford, D. (1991). *Influence without authority.* New York: John Wiley & Sons, Inc.

Hook, J. (1999). *The agile manager's guide to influencing people.* Bristol, VT: Velocity Business Publishing.

Johnson, R., & Eaton, J. (2002). *Influencing people.* London: Dorling Kindersley.

Maxwell, J., & Dornan, J. (1997). *Becoming a person of influence.* Atlanta, GA: Maxwell Motivation, Inc.

Pfeffer, J. (1992). *Managing with power: Politics and influence in organizations.* Boston: Harvard Business School Press.

Rogers, J. (1999). *Influencing people: The essential guide to thinking and working smarter.* New York: American Management Association.

Background

Research about how managers use influence has a long history and has led to a general understanding that leaders can use multiple tactics to build commitment and get results from peers, direct reports, and bosses. Focusing on the practices identified by researchers (Yukl & Falbe, 1990; Yukl, Lepsinger, & Lucia, 1992; Yukl & Tracey, 1992) and currently employed in organizations, CCL has developed several educational programs that focus on the art of influencing. Some of those programs bring participants to one of CCL's campuses to learn about and develop their influence skills, and others are created as custom developmental initiatives for specific clients who want to teach their employees the tactics for getting results in an era of flat organizations and multiple roles.

CCL uses assessment instruments, videotaped role-plays, and scripted vignettes to help managers uncover the influence tactics they use most often and those they need to develop to be more effective. In addition, participants in CCL's influence-focused programs gain awareness of and confidence about when to use certain influence tactics, which optimizes their social capital and interpersonal effectiveness. The educational initiative that most clearly focuses on the development of influence tactics is CCL's Foundations of Leadership program, and the topic ranks as one of the most sought-after subjects in CCL's custom leadership development programs.

Key Point Summary

Influence is an essential component of leadership. Your position in an organization and the power it gives you aren't always enough to motivate people to do what you ask. Developing your influence skills can help you gain commitment from people at all levels: direct reports, peers, and bosses.

Influence tactics may be logical, emotional, or cooperative. The first step is to assess the tactics you currently use. Then you can develop those you rarely use to become more effective.

Planning is important. Set your goals: determine what you want to accomplish and whom you need to influence. Consider any benefits and challenges you may have going into the situation so that you can capitalize on the benefits and address the challenges. Identify the influence tactics that are likely to work best. Pay special attention to the tactics you rarely use, and think about how you can develop them before the influence session.

When it's time for the actual dialogue, set the stage for your request and establish rapport with the other person. Use your plan to help you focus during the conversation. Capitalize on points of agreement to move toward your desired outcome.

Afterward, record what happened and think through what you have learned. In this way, every influence attempt becomes a learning experience, and you continue to enhance your capability.

Ordering Information

FOR MORE INFORMATION, TO ORDER OTHER IDEAS INTO ACTION GUIDEBOOKS, OR TO FIND OUT ABOUT BULK-ORDER DISCOUNTS, PLEASE CONTACT US BY PHONE AT 336-545-2810 OR VISIT OUR ONLINE BOOKSTORE AT WWW.CCL.ORG/GUIDEBOOKS. PREPAYMENT IS REQUIRED FOR ALL ORDERS UNDER $100.

Your Strength of Influence: A Self-Guided Worksheet
GRAPH

Plot each of your scores on the graph below and then connect the dots. This will show which influence tactics you can develop to be more effective.

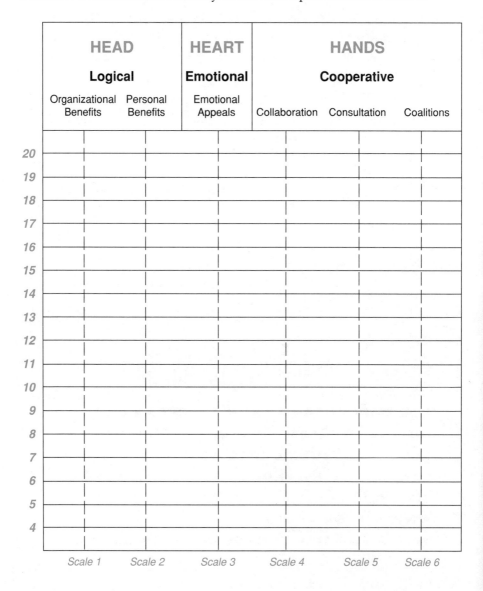